THE
SPIRITUAL
GIFTS
BLUEPRINT

THE
SPIRITUAL
GIFTS
BLUEPRINT

GOD'S DESIGN FOR YOUR GIFTS, TALENTS, AND PURPOSE

ANDY REESE

Chosen
a division of Baker Publishing Group
Minneapolis, Minnesota

© 2023 by Andrew J. Reese

Published by Chosen Books
Minneapolis, Minnesota
www.chosenbooks.com

Chosen Books is a division of
Baker Publishing Group, Grand Rapids, Michigan

Printed in the United States of America

Library of Congress Cataloging-in-Publication Data
Names: Reese, Andrew J., author.
Title: The spiritual gifts blueprint study guide : God's design for your gifts, talents, and purpose / Andy Reese.
Description: Minneapolis, Minnesota : Chosen Books, a division of Baker Publishing Group, 2023. | Includes bibliographical references.
Identifiers: LCCN 2023010165 | ISBN 9780800763534 (paperback) | ISBN 9781493442485 (ebook)
Subjects: LCSH: Gifts, Spiritual—Study and teaching. | Christian life. | Bible. Epistles of Paul—Criticism, interpretation, etc.
Classification: LCC BT767.3 .R442 2023 | DDC 234/.13—dc23/eng/20230527
LC record available at https://lccn.loc.gov/2023010165

Author is represented by Ambassador Literary Agency, Nashville, TN.

Baker Publishing Group publications use paper produced from sustainable forestry practices and post-consumer waste whenever possible.

23 24 25 26 27 28 29   7 6 5 4 3 2 1

I remind you to kindle afresh the gift of God which is in you. . . . For God has not given us a spirit of timidity, but of power and love and discipline.

2 Timothy 1:6–7

Contents

Hey, Friend,

You are gifted. I could even say that you are a "gifted child." Does that sound strange to you? Surely, I am talking about someone else, right? But God doesn't keep score as we do. He doesn't count achievement in terms of finances or followers. He simply says, "I perfectly formed and gifted you for a wonderful purpose, to be involved in certain things with Me. You are perfect for those things. Mistakes are fine. You're human! Let's find them together. Can't wait!"

For many years, I have had a burning passion to help people just like you understand the statement that God has an amazing and perfectly fitting purpose for them. And those things that have been prepared for your life can best be found along the path of your gifting. Finding that purpose is naturally supernatural. It is easy when we know there is such a thing. We simply say, "God, that is what I want to do and become. Will You help me?"

If that seems impossible or unreal, if you feel you are too old to start now, or whatever your reason or fear might be, I am here to tell and show you that His arms are open wide. It wasn't too late for the prodigal, the lost sheep, the thief on the cross, or Paul, the persecutor of believers. Never. Too. Late. Never over. It is just the beginning—new every morning.

Let's walk into this journey of connection and discovery together, growing more purposeful and more delighted. This study guide is designed to be used either alone or with others, and it is formatted to last eight weeks (although each week can be split into separate parts, which makes the total study length flexible).

Your brother and friend,

Andy

Understanding Where You Are

"I think only God can show me my gifting and purpose, and I don't know why He won't! Every answer I find seems to be unhelpful and contradicts every other answer. 'Spiritual gifts' seems to be sort of a Christian inside joke. I need answers. Where is God in all this anyway?"

The Spiritual Gifts Blueprint, chapter 1

Before you begin, please read chapter 1 of *The Spiritual Gifts Blueprint*.

The Main Thing

As you read chapter 1, notice that across the spectrum of church types and affiliations there is a large number of competing definitions and associated understandings of the term *spiritual gifts* and nothing at all about the various individual roles of the Trinity members. This situation has effectively clouded the probable intention of God that a clear understanding of our gifting and intimate connection, or co-working, with each member of the Trinity in their roles would serve a central place in our lives, guiding and accompanying us toward God's purposes for each—for you.

Individual Study

Your Story

The quote above came from the words of an angry and confused college student who was seeking direction in her life and feeling as though knowing her spiritual gifting would help. Your own feelings and words may be a bit like that. Maybe not. Let's explore your story from several directions to help you understand where you

11

feel you are now on the subject of spiritual gifts and connection with the Trinity.

Think back over your history as a believer. It may be long or short, fairly uncomplicated, or complex and jumbled. No matter. God isn't confused about you! When you look back on your story as a Christian who is gifted by God, see if you can recall and frame answers to these questions. "I'm not sure" is a fine answer.

1. *Where am I?* In chapter 1, we discussed a one-question survey I had two groups of college students take. Let's try it. On a scale of 1 to 5 (where 1 is "little knowledge or little interest," 3 is "an idea but little practical application," and 5 is "a pretty clear understanding and use of spiritual gifts"), how would you rate your current understanding, belief, and practice in the area of gifting—however you define it? Write a one-sentence description of your current stance (as reflected by your self-rating score) that someone else could read to gain an initial impression of where you are.

Look at the "spectrum" figure on page 24 in chapter 1. Do you see yourself somewhere along that spectrum? Describe your formative or current church affiliation, if any, and brief history:

2. *How did I get here?* In a sentence or two, think about and jot down the key relationships, events, or drivers for how you came to your current understanding or practice concerning spiritual gifting. For example, was it in a class, a church, a college Bible study, or did it come from a parent or a friend?

3. *How do I relate to "Gift Lists"?* Chapter 1, on pages 28 and 29, talks about different definition lists of *spiritual gifts*. Does your understanding of your spiritual gifts coincide with any listing source, particular teaching, or teacher with whom you are familiar? In your current understanding, how many spiritual gifts are there? What are their names? Do they come from a particular Bible passage?

Group Discussion

Shared Stories

If you are part of a group that is discussing the book, great! As we go along, I will note ways your group can share together your history and journey. Often the individual questions will be the best source for group sharing—and reading the book chapter(s) and individually responding to those questions ahead of the group gathering will be effective.

This first group discussion is a time to get to know each other, our stories, and our histories.

1. Encourage each group member to briefly share a summary of his or her answers to questions 1 and 2 (*Where am I?* and *How did I get here?*) above. Be sure that each member feels comfortable that there is no right or wrong answer. Allow questions for clarification and understanding.

2. Talk together about question 3 (above) and your current understanding of and experience with spiritual gifts. How do you currently see or define them?

3. Think about the following admonitions from Paul to Timothy:

   "Do not neglect the spiritual gift within you" (1 Timothy 4:14).

   "I remind you to kindle afresh the gift of God which is in you. . . . For God has not given us a spirit of timidity, but of power and love and discipline" (2 Timothy 1:6–7).

   Think about Paul's listing of the three complimentary understandings of the Holy Spirit and spiritual gifts: power, love, and sound, disciplined thinking (which is a fuller translation). How would you describe your current understanding or application of spiritual gifts from this three-part perspective? Which of the three seems most important in your own belief and practice of spiritual gifts? How might these three balancing aspects be used to keep this part of your life in proper balance?

4. Brainstorm together on potential ways that you can stir up your own gifting (as Paul admonished Timothy) and help support each other to do so.

5. Pray for each other that everyone in your group might know God's intention for gifting in their lives. Pray that you all would be mutually encouraged in the journey.

Understanding the Spirit Structure

The Corinthian Church, founded by Paul, apparently asked his advice on several issues, including the church's disorderly meetings and the misuse of manifestations of the Holy Spirit—specifically tongues and prophecy. Intended by God for good, the outcome was a cacophony of tongues without interpretation, prophecy without mature content judgment, and speaking on top of each other. Perhaps they had bigger issues.

The Spiritual Gifts Blueprint, chapter 2

Before you begin, please read chapter 2 of *The Spiritual Gifts Blueprint.*

Review of Last Session

Take a couple of minutes to review what you wrote in Session 1. Write one line describing something that stood out. Why did it stand out? If you're in a group, share what you wrote, and observe the similarities or differences among your group members. Jot down any additional insights you gained from the group.

The Main Thing

The Corinthian Church seemed to be a mess, at least when they met together. And Paul spent much of his first letter addressing the part of that mess that related to their misunderstanding and misdefining of spiritual gifts—and far more. They seemed ignorant of how the faith they professed and the God they served worked in and through them. Paul, probably addressing the question they *should*

15

have asked, summarizes a four-part spirit structure that seems carefully configured to be biblical, practical, God-connecting, and transformative. We may share some of that Corinthian ignorance and need. Let's go!

Individual Study

What Paul Said[1]

Here is Paul's initial response to that Corinthian ignorance. To avoid having to go back and forth between this workbook and *The Spiritual Gifts Blueprint*, I have copied 1 Corinthians 12:1–8 and 11 from the book (page 34) in the format as described there. Read slowly, and pay careful attention to the Greek words in brackets and note the first impressions or thoughts that enter your mind. Be on the alert for repeated words, patterns of thought, lists, mention of the Trinity, and whatever seems pertinent to your understanding. Scribble and highlight!

[1]Now, concerning things of the spirit [*pneumatikos*], brothers and sisters, I don't want you to be uninformed and ignorant. [4]There is a distinct division [*diairesis*] of grace-gifts [*charisma*], but the same Spirit. [5]There is a distinct division [*diairesis*] of ministries [*diakonia*], but the same Lord. [6]There is a distinct division [*diairesis*] of empowered effects [*energema*], but the same God who works all things in everyone. [7]On the other hand, each one is given the clearly visible manifestation [*phanerosis*] of the Spirit for the common good. [8]For to one is given [the nine manifestations of the Spirit are listed by Paul here]. . . . [11]But the same Spirit empowers these things distinctly dividing [*diairesis*] to each individually as He wills.

1. NOTE: I will briefly summarize Greek word meanings throughout the book; however, you might be interested in doing a little simple and enlightening additional legwork yourself. Don't be intimidated, we are not translating, but simply seeking to know various ways scholars have seen things. I recommend the best website to use for this purpose is Bible Hub (www.biblehub.com). Within ten minutes you'll be seeing your focus verses in multiple parallel translations, perusing Greek words and their various meanings, reading commentary thoughts, and more. You might get hooked. Get coffee!

Paul's Patterns and Words

Let's carefully try to sort out the truth Paul conveys. Why might this be important? This is Paul's response to the Corinthian ignorance and disorder. Note that the word in verse 1 that is often translated *spiritual gifts* is actually a word with far wider meaning. It might be better translated (and is translated here) as "things of the spirit." Paul, in a few short verses, shares a compact and comprehensive understanding and deep-truth pattern about the spirit world that goes well beyond *spiritual gifts*.

There are different approaches to considering these verses that ultimately lead to different interpretations of what Paul is saying. And those interpretations then ripple through Christian belief and practice and can have an impact on our lives. In these verses, as noted in the book, Paul uses a Greek word describing a logic process, *diairesis*, four times to describe his approach to understanding the parts of this topic.

Here is an interesting quote from Plato (the probable inventor of this *diairesis* thought process) on what happens when one does *not* take into account the thorough logic, formally or informally, involved in using a *diairesis* thought process.

> Because people are not in the habit of considering things by dividing them into classes [*diairesis*], they hastily put these widely different relations into the same category, thinking they are alike; and again they do the opposite of this when they fail to divide other things into parts.[2]

It seems to make sense that we give Paul the benefit of the doubt and start with the assumption that the unique word he repeats four times (*diairesis*) regarding how he went about consideration of each of these four things of the spirit (*pneumatikos*) has important implications for our understanding far beyond spiritual gifts. Overlooking what he may be saying might have led directly to the Corinthian confusion described in chapter 1, and it may have helped create any confusion you too may be feeling.

I have divided our discussion into three related concepts: Pneumatikos Thinking, The Four-Part Spirit Structure, and Diairesis Thinking.

All in? Let's explore together.

2. Plato, *The Statesman*, 285a.

Pneumatikos Thinking

The first place to start sorting things out is at the very beginning. Look at verse 1 above. If you have access to an app, such as Bible Hub, look at that verse in several translations. Paul introduces his argument saying, "Now, concerning *pneumatikos*, brothers and sisters, I don't want you to be uninformed and ignorant." Seems innocent right? Well . . .

1. In 1 Corinthians 12:1, how is the Greek word *pneumatikos* translated in your Bible? What if you look at other versions?

    That word, *pneumatikos,* in a Christian context means "spiritual" or "things of the spirit." This means Paul is actually saying, "Now concerning things of the spirit."

    As you probably saw if you were able to look at that verse in different translations, many translators have translated that word as "spiritual gifts." Others have added the word "gifts" after "spiritual" and placed it in italics. Italics indicate that the word "gifts" is not actually present in the original Greek but was thought to be helpful by the translators. Only the more literal translations (e.g., Young's Literal Translation or the World English Bible) do not include "gifts" but translate the word as "spiritual things." In every other use of the word *pneumatikos* in Scripture, the "gifts" addition is not there.

2. Why do you think some translators have added the word "gifts"?

3. In a sentence or two, if you were to translate 1 Corinthians 12:1 to the more accurate and broader term "now

concerning things of the spirit" or the "structure of the spirit," instead of the narrower focus of "now concerning spiritual gifts," how might that change your consideration and understanding of the rest of the paragraph?

Let's move to the next big idea in Paul's writing in 1 Corinthians 12: the four-part structure of the spirit (*pneumatikos*) world.

Diairesis Thinking

"There is a distinct division [*diairesis*] of . . ." Each time Paul lists a component of the four parts of the spirit structure (*pneumatikos*) and a corresponding member of the Trinity (discussed next), he states there is a *diairesis* way of thinking about it. What does that mean?

Reread the discussion of Paul's *diairesis* in chapter 2 as described on pages 37–40 of the book. *Diairesis* can be defined as "a distinction arising from a different distribution to different persons." It can be thought of as a three-step process to carefully consider some topic: 1) define the overall topic of analysis; 2) consider how to define and title the complete range of possible "class" members within that topic; and, 3) based on the specific purpose of the *diairesis* analysis, think deeply about each of the categories, patterns, uses, order, meaning, etc., in terms of some final decision, distribution, or disposition.

1. Recall that the only other use of *diairesis* is the father of both the prodigal and older brother who carefully divided his estate between the two brothers. How would you describe what *diairesis* thinking might look like in that situation?

2. What might implications of this *diairesis* thought process be for anyone learning or teaching on this topic of spiritual gifts and things of the spirit?

3. What differences in our thinking might occur if we miss the point that Paul's lists are probably meant to thoroughly define a topic top-to-bottom and end-to-end *diairesis* style? What if I assume that Paul's lists are merely examples of some much larger (maybe infinite) list of gifts not given in Scripture?

The Four-Part Spirit Structure

The third place to look for truth about what Paul is saying is to notice the word-pattern repeated four times (see verses 4, 5, 6, 8, 11) in the verses above. Each of the four parts has this identical pattern: (1) the word *diairesis* (discussed above); (2) a different component of the spirit structure (gifts, ministries, energizings, and manifestations); and (3) a matching member of the Trinity who apparently has a special association with that particular component.

1. Fill in this table for the four components and use a few words to define that component of the spirit structure (refer to pages 35–37 in the book for help with the definitions):

Component	Component Greek Word	Component English Word	Associated Trinity Member	Brief Definition
1				
2				
3				
4				

2. If this analysis of things of the spirit (*pneumatikos*) is Paul's overall top level *diairesis* analysis on this subject, then what are some things that might imply about these four topics?

Group Discussion

This second group discussion is a time to explore each other's understanding and impressions from chapter 2.

1. Encourage each group member to briefly share a summary of his or her answers to questions 1–3 under Pneumatikos Thinking. Ensure that each member feels comfortable that

there is no right or wrong answer. Allow questions for clarification and understanding.

2. How does this four-part understanding of things of the spirit compare to your understanding of these verses coming into this study? How might the concept of *diairesis* analysis factor into the four-part structure of things of the spirit? Is there some part of either this approach or your past approach that doesn't make sense to you? Discuss those together.

3. Why do you think Paul has linked each of the four parts of the structure of the spirit (*pneumatikos*) to a different member of the Trinity? Was he simply waxing poetic, or are there ways that a realization of this linkage to a Trinity member might change the way you think about and walk out various parts of your Christian faith?

4. As you think about the roles of each member of the Trinity in your life, try to recall a time or an event when it seems clear (possibly in retrospect) that a particular member of the Trinity was at work on your behalf. Share those times or events.

5. Pray for each other that all in your group might know God's intention for gifting in their lives and grow in their connection with each member of the Trinity.

The Structure of Charisma Gifts

He is one who leads. He can't help it. God wants you to understand and live in your gifting. You can't help it, either. And because God is active in bringing you into the power of your gifting, even with a limited amount of understanding, when you simply do what seems right—that which captures your attention, turns your head, or maybe makes your blood boil—then you will stumble into your gifting. This will happen even if you aren't sure it is a "thing" and certainly could never name it. Oh, the Father's mercy!

The Spiritual Gifts Blueprint, chapter 3

Before you begin, read chapter 3 of *The Spiritual Gifts Blueprint.*

Review of Last Session

Take a couple minutes to review what you wrote in Session 2. Write one line that describes something that stood out. If you're in a group, share what you wrote, and observe the similarities or differences among your group's comments. Jot down any additional insights you gained from the group.

The Main Thing

The quote above is from chapter 3 of the book. It is a story about a young man who was moved to use his gifting (though he would not have recognized those terms) to organize and lead in a fast-paced tornado recovery—with an interesting mix of volunteers! It's important to understand that in that same emergency, there could have been a story about you, too. You may be quieter or you may be different, but you, too, can't help being who you are. And sometimes, in times when careful self-control and normal daily duties go out the window, our gifting emerges. The streets were filled with quiet servants with chainsaws.

Your *charisma* gift is a big part of you, too. Understanding that and what your gifting might be are both keys to far more easily finding God's purposes for your life and the deep satisfaction and sense of getting traction that brings.

Because this is an approach that differs in some ways from convention, even though it is biblical, practical, God-connecting, and transformational, I want to take two sections in this study guide to explore it in detail. These two sections will match chapters 3 and 4 of the book. In this section of the Study Guide, let's look together at our *charisma* gifting as explained in chapter 3 of the book. We will gain the background keys we need to unlock our gifting in chapter 4.

Individual Study

Paul and Peter's Keys to Charisma Gifting

I'll explain more in Session 7 about the place of the nine manifestations of the Holy Spirit listed by Paul in 1 Corinthians 12:8–10, and the confusion with the term *charisma* gifts in Paul's *pneumatikos* spiritual structure. For now, however, let's go with the idea that *charisma* gifts are the topic of both Peter's description in 1 Peter 4:10–11 and Paul's listing of the seven such gifts in Romans 12:3–8, because that is what they specifically call them.

Carefully read Peter's description and then Paul's description of *charisma* gifts that are printed below. Notice how Peter and Paul enhance but do not contradict each other.

Consider yourself a detective looking for clues, patterns, and connections between the two descriptions of *charisma*. Get a pencil and highlighter and spend some time exploring. Draw arrows, highlight similar things with the same color, and scribble! In the space below the Scripture passages, jot down titles and one-line descriptions of each key point you notice: facts, implications, similarities, lists, categories, differences, truths, etc.

Okay, Sherlock. It's all yours!

Peter on Charisma Gifts (1 Peter 4:10–11)

As each one has received a special gift [*charisma*], employ it in serving [*diakonia*] one another as good stewards of the multifaceted [*poikilos*] grace of God. Whoever speaks is to do so as one who is speaking actual words of God; whoever serves is to do so as one who is serving by the strength which God supplies; so that in all things God may be glorified through Jesus Christ, to whom belongs the glory and dominion forever and ever. Amen.

Paul on Charisma Gifts (Romans 12:6–8)

Since we have gifts [*charisma*] that differ according to the grace [*charis*] given to us, each of us is to use them properly: if prophecy, in proportion to one's faith; if service, in the act of serving; or the one who teaches, in the act of teaching; or the one who exhorts, in the work of exhortation; the one who gives, with generosity; the one who is in leadership, with diligence; the one who shows mercy, with cheerfulness.

Here is the spot to jot down a one-line description of each key thing you notice and its address(es):

1. _____

   _____

2. _____

   _____

When you're done, take a look at the seven keys my own detective work found that are listed below and are described in chapter 3 of the book. How many did you find? How many did I miss? How would you describe the same key but with a different slant?

We will save Keys 8 and 9 for the next chapter, because they are more logically derived conclusions and derivations from Peter and Paul's descriptions, pertinent to the Gift Circle that is coming up next.

Key 1: There Are Seven Charisma Gifts in Two General Categories
- These seven cover every need in the Body.

Key 2: We Each Have a Gift
- We may not know what it is, but no one is without a *charisma* gift.

Key 3: Our Gift Is Our General Function in the Body
- Every believer is given a basic motivation in the Body, and that motivation supports our Body function (discussed in Session 5).

Key 4: We Have One Charisma Gift
- The hand cannot suddenly become a foot—that is bad science fiction.

Key 5: We Are Stewards Serving, Not Owners Presiding
- My *charisma* gift is just that—a gift.

Key 6: Our Gift Is Not Our Identity
- God looks at and loves *us*, not our gifting. We each are "one who" does some function. He loves the "one."

Key 7: Our Gifts Are Empowered by God
- They are not human talents, but God's anointing for a certain partnership function.

Group Discussion

This third group discussion is a time to explore each other's understanding and impressions from the above Scripture passages and how they might apply in our lives. This discussion may take more than one gathering time.

1. Take turns going around to each group member.
   - Encourage each group member to briefly share one of the keys they found and their one-line description.
   - Others who found the same key (or nearly the same) should add their thoughts and insights before the next turn is taken.
   - If that key is similar to one on the list I have given, look at the similarities and differences.
   - Share together ideas about how that key might apply in life or how it might change and enhance one's understanding of a biblical truth.
   - Note additions or observations that enhance your individual responses above.

2. Once you have completed discussion of your own keys, look at the remainder of the list I have provided. Discuss those additional keys as in step 1.

3. As you think about these keys and how they might apply to your life, try to recall a time or an event when it seemed clear (possibly in retrospect) that a particular key was in action. Discuss together those times or events.

4. Pray for each other that all in your group might know God's intention for gifting in their lives.

Understanding
Your Charisma Gift

After a brief explanation, I asked the group to walk around on a "shopping" stroll. I asked them to feel and think, to determine which of the poster descriptions seemed most like them. I cautioned them not to think too hard or to second guess their decision too much—to ask their mates if they were stuck! I also instructed them that after they decided, they should grab a chair and sit in front of that poster. . . . An amazing thing happened. The murmur of talk slowly grew into a laughing cacophony. Heads nodded, backs were slapped, and fist were bumped all around the room. When the stories began, there were tears and hugs—like finding a lost family.

The Spiritual Gifts Blueprint, chapter 4

Before you begin, read chapter 4 of *The Spiritual Gifts Blueprint*.

Review of Last Session

Take a couple of minutes to review what you wrote in Session 3. Write one line describing something that stood out. Why did it stand out? If you're in a group, share what you wrote, and observe the similarities or differences among your group's comments. Jot down any additional insights you gained from the group.

The Main Thing

As stated previously, understanding your *charisma* gifting is foundational to finding purpose, because the purposes of God seem to make use of His primary gifting within each of us. That makes sense.

Finding that gifting is not difficult. Across the Church, however, it has often felt that way. In some places, it might even feel irrelevant, given all the conflicting definitions. But that is on us. We, not God, have made it so. God is all in on creating simple ways of helping you zero in on your gifting; especially if your desire is to use it to carry out His purposes for your life. In this section, we will focus on you—your God-given *charisma* gifting. I hope that you come away saying, "I think my gifting is like this. At least, I'm pretty sure it is. I'm going to go on that assumption and see where God leads." Let's do it!

Individual Study

Gift Circle Understanding

Recall that in chapter 3 of the book, I derived and described logically the biblical idea that Paul and Peter defined the seven "primary colors" of *charisma* gifts. When looked at together, those seven gifts cover the myriad of variations of the gifting of every Christian on earth, the same way the seven basic colors of the rainbow represent all the visible colors in the spectrum. If this is so, then a number of simplifying approaches can be developed, including the Gift Circle. Let's go there.

The quote at the beginning of this section describes an amazing morning in a Sunday School class in which the Gift Circle was accidentally created. It has since proven to be a very useful tool in helping people just like you begin to get a good idea of the nature of their spiritual gifting—that is, their *charisma* gift "arc" in the Circle.

The figure below is the Gift Circle.[1] Let's first make sure you have a clear picture of how the *charisma* gifts are envisioned through this tool.

---

1. The diagram is in black and white, but a color version is available at https://andyreese.org/about-us.

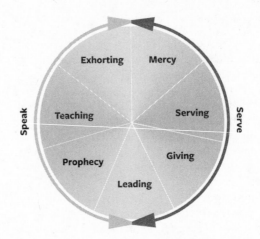

Here is a set of one-line title statements about the Gift Circle that are each explained in more detail in chapter 4 of the book. Summarize your understanding in a brief explanation of each title and why it might be important. In a group setting, you can work through these together sharing thoughts and ideas. Feel free to refer to the chapter to ensure you gain a clear understanding of each concept before we apply them to our giftings.

1. There are no actual internal boundaries.
   Meaning:

   Importance:

2. We each occupy an "arc" in the circle.
   Meaning:

Importance:

3. There is an infinite number of individual *charisma* gift arcs.
   Meaning:

   Importance:

4. We each are mostly one thing—our arc is mostly within one
   gift title.
   Meaning:

   Importance:

5. We can "visit" giftings but live in one place.
   Meaning:

   Importance:

6. Speaking and serving gifts motivationally "match" across the circle.

Meaning:

Importance:

Finding My Charisma Gift

It seems that there are two related ways to make an initial determination of your *charisma* gift. The first is a straightforward review of descriptions of each of the seven, and then simply recognizing or sensing which one, or adjacent gift combination, seems to fit best. This might best be done with friends. Elbowing is allowed! The second way involves envisioning situations and answering "what if" questions.

Method 1: Review of the Seven Charisma Gifts

In the book and with the locations listed below, I provide three different detailed levels of *charisma* gift descriptions that are useful in different settings. Use whichever approach works best in the situation you are in.

- Chapter 3 Key 1 page 48 (and used in the exercise below) for quick reference is a set of one-line descriptions of the seven. This list provides what kind of issue the gift addresses and what it produces in its place.
- Chapter 4 page 67 begins a more detailed narrative description of each of the seven. It is useful for giving someone a feel for the gift without needing to check off a list of features or characteristics.
- Appendix B page 196 introduces the posters used in the Sunday class described at the beginning of chapter 4. Each poster has multiple characteristics from many sources that

are merged into a fairly comprehensive set of "what to look for" in someone who may have that particular gift. Typically, if someone is really stuck, something on that list will make them smile, nod, and say, "Well okay, then!"

Here is a one-line "purpose" description of each of the seven. I have provided the "target" of each gift and left a blank for what the gift is motivated to accomplish in place of the negative. See how many you can recall or determine. When you have gone as far as you are able, look on page 65 for my version of what each is motivated to bring about.

Leading—eliminating group dysfunction and bringing

___

Prophecy—eliminating what is wrong and bringing

___

Teaching—eliminating what is ignorant or false and bringing

___

Exhorting—eliminating wounding and confusion and bringing

___

Giving—eliminating lack and investing in

___

Serving—eliminating physical needs and focusing on

___

Mercy—eliminating pain and sadness and bringing

___

◈ Method 2: The Three Steps

This second approach (taken from chapter 4 beginning on page 73) is a method that was developed for various student and church lectures. While it is not perfect, it is valuable in sorting out if your gifting is primarily in the speaking or serving category and which of the three in each category you might see as your primary arc. It is a three-step exercise (with an application at the end) designed to help you envision your gifting. I say envision because, at least in my experience, gifts are normally sensed and felt first with reason following. If I think too hard, I can come up with reasons I could do any (or none) of the gifts.

The three steps are given on pages 73–76 and are partially reproduced here.

Step 1—Is my primary gift area speaking or serving?

Someone comes to you and says, "Hey, I was wondering if you'd be willing to give a twenty-minute speech on some topic of interest to you at the City Council meeting this Friday. I know it is Wednesday, but the other speaker cancelled. They try to have a local person give an interesting talk once a quarter. Maybe one hundred people will be there—probably the mayor, too. Oh, it will be televised."

Picture the continuum of feelings you might experience when asked that question. On one end is total mortification. On the other end is probably some form of ignorant overconfidence. Without thinking too hard (which might change your initial emotion), where are you along that continuum? Do others agree? Why or why not?

Where Are You?

1. If you are sure that you are not a public speaker and feel unwilling (left side) and your friends or mate seem to agree with that assessment, then you should be thinking of your primary *charisma* gifting being in the *serving* family of gifts. Skim step 2 and go to step 3.

2. If, on the other hand, even with a nervous feeling, excitement rises inside and you get a sense of actually doing that, then you should be thinking of your primary *charisma* gifting being in the *speaking* family of gifts. Go to step 2.

Summarize the outcome of step 1 and share any feelings or thoughts that came to you that seemed to clinch the deal. Understand that childhood wounding or discouragement might influence your courage in this step. If that might be you, ask friends to help you think this through.

Step 2—If my primary gift area seemed to be *speaking*, which of the three might be the biggest part of the arc?

If you were given *one* chance to speak to your church on a Sunday morning, or to a group or company, would your focus or motivation tend to be centered more on approach A, B, or C below? Look inside yourself and find which emotion, motivation, and direction seem to outweigh any other. Here is what I wrote in the book on pages 73–74.

A. You are complimentary to them, but also feel an itch toward being gently corrective to help them be the best they can be ("I think we're missing something here!"). Perhaps it is about a great opportunity they could, or should, be doing something about or doing better in it. It might feel as if you were bringing up something that needs to be improved or redirected—maybe bringing up a need they might be overlooking.

B. You are excited to tell them about an amazing truth you found in Scripture that had an impact on your life ("I just have to show you this pattern in Romans that is so interesting and applicable to us."). Maybe it is something you found that they might find exciting or transformative. For a work group, it might mean sharing some pertinent company improvement training that you have found to be applicable or informational in a way that you hope will be insightful and helpful. You are bringing important information.

C. You seem to have a clear vision about the strengths and calling of the church or group, and you want to encourage them regarding their amazing abilities or history ("You guys are amazing in something and I'm going to tell you all about it!"). You encourage them when you speak about God's love, provision, and protection. You might share specifically about growing opportunities and how they can walk more fully in them. Or for an organization, you encourage them regarding the strengths and possibilities within the firm or organization. You describe a realistically great path forward and urge them to be their best selves and go for it. You are encouraging and exhorting.

The first (A) would point toward a *prophecy* gifting—seeing a correction or a shortfall that you have trouble simply ignoring. The second (B) would indicate a *teaching* gifting—being excited to illustrate and apply biblical truth. And the third (C) would indicate an *exhorting* gifting—being excited about who someone is and what God has put inside of them.

Write down and share your thoughts on this step. Try to explain your feelings and drives. Did you feel that there might be some overlap between Teaching and Prophecy or Exhorting? Discuss with friends to see if they think you might lean to one side or the other of a particular speaking gift. Why do they think that?

Summarize the outcome of step 2; share any feelings or thoughts that came to you that seemed to clinch the deal.

Step 3—If my primary gift area seemed to be *serving*, which of the three might be the biggest part of the arc?

Recall the scenario in the restaurant given in the book on page 75:

You are a uniformed server in a fancy restaurant that has a big table of businesspeople celebrating a corporate year-end success. You and several others are handling that table. The restaurant is busy, drinks are very late, and the table is growing restless and impatient. A young server on your team finally emerges from the kitchen with a tray loaded with long-overdue fancy drink orders. But the server forgets there is a step down to the table and slips slightly, the tray becomes unbalanced, tilts, and spills all the drinks on the floor with a crash, a splash, and a clatter. It all seems to happen in slow motion as you freeze in horrified shock. The restaurant hushes. The table looks on with impatient disgust. You are standing there. Close your eyes and imagine that situation, see it, and feel it.

Here is the question: Without overthinking, what do you feel an immediate urge to do? You feel you must . . .

- Go straight to the mess ("It's a *mess!!*"), urgently needing to get things orderly and cleaned up before somebody steps on the glass or slips on the splattered puddle.
- Go straight to the person ("Oh, my poor friend!!"), bringing comforting words to defuse the embarrassment they surely feel and offering your emotional support in whatever way they most need.
- Go straight to the kitchen ("They need drinks, and fast!!") to get new drink orders going, knowing the table is waiting impatiently and feeling a need to serve the clients, meet the need for drinks, and cover the restaurant's reputation.

The desperate need to clean up the mess (A) would point toward *serving* as the primary focus of your gifting. The sudden strong concern for your fellow server (B) would indicate *mercy*. And the need to get those amazing drinks (probably comped) to the people who ordered them (C) would tend to indicate *giving* as your primary gift. (What do your friends think you would do and why? Do they have stories?)

As with the speaking gifts, it would be good to think about this scenario, pay attention to your inner motivation in various situations, and let it seep into you over the next months. Review the Gift Circle and descriptions, with an arc in mind, to see whether an adjacent gifting seems pertinent in terms of "coloring" your primary gift as explained in the book. Ask God for insight. Pay attention to nudges and simple one-shot opportunities to step in and let your gifting flow. (And get coffee with friends and talk it over.)

To make that process easier, provide a recap of your feelings and the thoughts that led you to that choice (without rethinking and analyzing it!).

The Leader—Somebody needs to organize all this!

If all you want to do is to step in and shout orders to the slow and confused wait staff, or, more calmly, you think about all the speaking or serving responses above and say to yourself, "Well, I could do any of those. But really, if the organization is inefficient and ineffective, then these things are of secondary importance," then you might be "one who leads." That is their classic response. (Talk to others about that feeling and ask them what they think.)

Recap your feelings and thoughts that led you to the "one who leads" conclusion:

Growing in Understanding about My Gift

Okay. How are you feeling? Don't overthink it or make it hard. If it is His will for us to understand and walk in our gifting, how hard can it be?

Remember that our knowledge of our gifting area comes with connected experience, not simply studying or taking a test—trial and error and success, and a growing inner joy at the connection and growing lifestyle change. And patience.

Jot down any stray thoughts, events, conversations, etc., that influence your thinking:

Recap the outcome of the three-step process:

Group Discussion

This fourth group discussion is a time to explore the sense each has of their own gifting. It is how they might continue to explore their understanding of their gifting and apply it in their lives.

The Gift Circle Components

Share together each person's response to the Individual Study section above concerning understanding of the six key concepts that went into creation of the Gift Circle. Jot down insights shared by others.

1. There are no actual internal boundaries.

2. We each occupy an "arc" in the circle.

3. There is an infinite number of individual *charisma* gift arcs.

4. We each are mostly one thing—our arc is mostly within one gift title.

5. We can "visit" giftings, but we live in one place.

6. Speaking and serving gifts motivationally "match" across the circle.

Finding My Charisma Gift—Gift Definitions

Recall that there are two common methods of finding my gift: reading and discussing the definitions, and the three steps. In the Individual Study section, to assist in Method 1 (reading gift definitions), I provided three different detail levels for defining *charisma* gifts.

- Chapter 3 Key 1 (page 48)—one-line descriptions of the seven.

- Chapter 4 (pages 67–70)—brief narrative description of each of the seven.
- Appendix B (pages 196–204)—the posters.

In a group setting, you can do this one at a time with your group members helping you think it through. Each person, in turn, tries to answer the questions with input (and probably jokes and stories!) from others. For some, having others recognizing that special thing about them is what they really need to begin to step into it. The discussion should be supportive. Group members should give suggestions and friendly observations for individual consideration but should never steer or dictate.

Finding My Charisma Gift—The Steps

To ensure that all members share a common understanding of the technique, a group member should present the steps and lead a brief familiarization discussion.

1. There are several ways to use this information in a group setting:
   - Look at the steps together, sequentially going around the room and briefly walking each person through the steps as other group members encourage and comment on the strengths they see in that person.
   - Have an individual present his or her walk through the steps as an example to encourage the others.
   - Have each one share his or her walk, gaining supportive feedback from group members on the strengths they see in that person.

2. If someone has not done the exercise but is willing to walk through it with the group, someone else should serve as the facilitator and help them walk through the three steps.

3. Every person should write down their insights about their gifting and supporting information.

4. Discuss, talk, pray, and watch steps for the group members. Support each other and help each other gain deeper insight and understanding of their gifting. Connect with God throughout the week. Write down insights and thoughts to share with the group in a later meeting.

5. Pray for each other that all in your group might know God's intention for gifting in their lives.

Jesus and Ministry

Your Kingdom career path will change and mature over time—as will you. And at some point, a growing sense of a plan, purpose, and vision will emerge and mature. Understanding that this dynamic is real, is God-given, and is actually happening is important. In God's eyes, it is not a random walk. It is purposeful and planned.

The Spiritual Gifts Blueprint, chapter 5

Before you begin, please read chapters 5 and 6 of *The Spiritual Gifts Blueprint*.

Review of Last Session

Take a couple of minutes to review what you wrote in Session 4. Write one line that describes something that stood out to you. If you're in a group, share what you wrote, and observe the similarities or differences among your group's comments. Jot down any additional insights you gained from the group.

The Main Thing

The second "leg on the table" of the four-part spirit structure, laid out by Paul in 1 Corinthians 12, is Jesus and ministry. Recall that Paul wrote in verse 5, "There is a distinct division of ministries, but the same Lord." Chapters 5 and 6 of the book cover this aspect of the grace package of God for each of us. *Diakonia* is the Greek word translated "ministry" and relates to all kinds of ministering with and for God in both speaking and serving roles. It refers to both our current role and our long-term career path.

Individual Study

Giftings and Manifestations in the Body

The book states that finding our *charisma* gift helps us sense and be drawn to individual ministry-type activities. Eventually, it leads us to our basic career path within the Body. And it is that Body of Christ, active in both relationships and in the world, where the action involving gifting and manifestations of the Spirit takes place—just like when Jesus was physically on the earth. Let's take a look.

Romans 12:3–5

Take a look at Paul's stage-setting discussion of Christ's Body preceding the listing of *charisma* gifts.

> ³For through the grace given to me I say to everyone among you not to think more highly of himself than he ought to think; but to think so as to have sound judgment, as God has allotted to each a measure of faith. ⁴For just as we have many parts in one body and all the body's parts do not have the same function, ⁵so we, who are many, are one body in Christ, and individually parts of one another.⁶ However, since we have gifts [*charisma*] that differ . . .
>
> Romans 12:3–6

1. What does Paul say about the Body of Christ in these verses? What is the name he gives to our "job" in the Body in verse 4? What does that name imply?

45

2. In verse 6 Paul shifts to a specific listing of the seven *charisma* gifts. Based on these verses, what are your thoughts on how "function/body part" and "*charisma* gift" relate?

● **1 Corinthians 12:7–11 and 12–27**

Read the above verses in your Bible and keep your finger there as you look at the following questions. In verses 7–11, Paul gives his list of the nine manifestations of the Spirit (*phanerosis*) and states that the Spirit distributes (*diairesis*) to each as He wills. Then, as in Romans above, in verses 12–27, Paul switches gears (this time from the manifestation [*pneumatikos*] part to the Body of Christ discussion rather than the other way around as in the Romans verses) and goes on at length, and from several angles, with a discussion of the Body of Christ and each one's role in it.

Let's explore what he says that creates a healthy atmosphere for healthy body life and the manifestations to flourish. As you read through 1 Corinthians 12:12–27 in your Bible, work through the following questions list:

1. Make a one- or two-word listing (with verse numbers) of the different kinds of *unhealthy* attitudes Paul describes. Give each of those attitudes a title.

2. Make a one- or two-word listing (with verse numbers) of the *facts* about the Body that Paul gives.

3. Make a one- or two-word listing (with verse numbers) of *healthy attitudes or actions* the Body should take to preserve unity. Also, give each of those attitudes a title.

Summary: Look back over what you discovered concerning the Body of Christ as well as giftings (in Romans) and manifestations (in 1 Corinthians). Can you make a one- or two-sentence statement of truth on that topic that would serve to guide your thinking or actions in these two areas that are connected to the Holy Spirit?

• Paul's Ephesians 4 Analysis of Ministry

Chapter 5 describes Paul's Ephesians 4 intertwined and multi-faceted *diairesis* analysis of how ministry works, both within the

Church and among us as the Body of Christ. Five specific keys were "untangled" and described in chapter 4 that form a basis and structure for understanding Jesus and ministry. Let's make sure we have a good grasp of them and their importance.

Key 1: The Two Unities (verses 3 and 13)

1. Describe this key in your own words. What do the *unities* look like, and how would you recognize them? How do they differ from each other? What characteristics might indicate they are not fully present in a particular church?

2. How might this key affect how you view and interact with your local church?

Key 2: The Gift of Christ (verse 7)

1. What surprised you about this key and Paul's concept?

2. How would an understanding of Christ as the "brain" even more than as the "boss" of the Body change your understanding of how He works within you and your church or group?

Key 3: The Measure of Christ (verses 7, 13, and 16)

1. Describe the three uses of the word *measure* (*metron*) in this passage. How do they work together to build the Body?

2. How might this understanding change the concept of your role in the Body of Christ—and of the role of others?

3. How might this understanding provide a new understanding of some of Christ's parables like the "talents" or "minas" in Matthew 25:14–30 and Luke 19:11–27?

Key 4: The Equippers (verses 11 and 12)

1. Review the descriptions of each of the equippers in chapter 6. In a few words, define the primary task of each equipper.

2. Can you identify people who play some of these roles in your local congregation? Which equippers and their equipping roles seem to be missing, and how might a church suffer because of that?

3. How might understanding these equippers change the way a church "pastor" might operate? How might that change some of the expectations placed on him or her?

Key 5: Ligament Relationships (verses 15 and 16)

1. We all know connection is important in many ways. It is common to hear that the reason a person stays or leaves a local congregation has to do with connection. What important functions of connection can you identify in this passage?

2. Define the secret of church body growth in one sentence from key 5.

Introduction to Finding My Diakonia (Ministry)

Part 2 of chapter 6 (starting on page 100) describes how I might go about "finding my *diakonia* ministry." Based on that section, think about the following questions:

1. Why might the whole idea of "finding my ministry" be somewhat of an incorrect focus?

2. How might you redefine the idea of "finding my ministry" to something more in keeping with the words and ways of Christ?

Connecting with Jesus and His Word

Scripture is clear (as explained in chapter 2) that each member of the Trinity is in and with us, and each has a different role. The Spirit is associated with *charisma* gifts and manifestations. Jesus is associated with *diakonia* ministries (this chapter). And the Father is associated with causing things to happen through resourcing and guiding (*energema*) in all of life.

Here are five scriptural examples that help frame the current role of Jesus in His own words. Write your thoughts on Jesus as the head (brain) of the body, and how that particular verse might practically feel or look in your life.

1. "Teaching them to follow all that I have commanded you; and behold, I am with you always, to the end of the age" (Matthew 28:20).

2. "For where two or three have gathered in My name, I am there in their midst" (Matthew 18:20).

3. "I have been crucified with Christ; and it is no longer I who live, but Christ lives in me; and the life which I now live in the flesh I live by faith in the Son of God, who loved me and gave Himself up for me" (Galatians 2:20).

4. "I can do all things through Him who strengthens me" (Philippians 4:13).

5. "For this purpose I also labor, striving according to His power which works mightily within me" (Colossians 1:29).

Meditation on the Parables—General Guidance

I stated in the book under the third key in Ephesians 4 (the measure of Christ) that it is important to understand the desires and ways of Jesus to get to know Him intimately. He had a lot to say about those things in His teaching, and especially His parables. Within them are deep layers of meaning and hidden patterns. The section of the book entitled "Connecting with Jesus and His Word" (page 101) leads and encourages us to do just that—to soak in the teachings of Jesus and let them seep deeply into us. They transform our thinking and our lives. For each of the parables listed below, I encourage you to follow these steps:

1. Take a minute to still your mind and ask Jesus if it would be okay if you and He sat together to look at what He said. Take a deep breath. If you struggle with that process, take a minute to read Psalm 23 very slowly and, on the inner screen of impression and imagination in your mind, as David did, seek Him as the Shepherd who sits with you beside quiet waters at a table in the presence of everything that would want to distract you.

2. When you feel the beginning of that stillness, read the first part of the parable slowly—part by part, like sipping an amazing drink prepared especially for you. Try to see it and feel it. Ask Jesus to show you where He is in it and what He wants you to know and see. Soak in it.

3. Let the words take on life and have deeper meaning for you. Pay attention to thoughts, memories, feelings, and pictures.

4. Move to the next part of the parable when you're ready.

5. When you finish, ask Jesus if there is anything else He wants to show you, teach you, or say to you. Listen. Jot down a few words that will later remind you of what you experienced. See below for specific questions for each parable.

The Sower and the Seed *(Matthew 13:1–23; Mark 4:1–20; Luke 8:4–15)*

1. Jesus, do I have characteristics of different soils? If so, can You show me?

2. Jesus, would You show me what I need to know about the next correct step in dealing with any unattractive characteristics and building the "good soil" character within me?

The Talents and the Minas *(Matthew 25:14–30; Luke 19:11–27)*

1. Jesus, would You show me what I need to see about describing the "talents" or "minas" that You have given to me?

2. Are there any ways I am burying them? If so, can You show me why?

The Seed *(Mark 4:26–29)*

1. Jesus, where have I already planted good seed? Will You help me be patient and faithful in waiting?

2. Is there an area in my life in which I need to till and plant good seed?

The Shrewd Servant *(Luke 16:1–13)*

1. Jesus, will You show me what has been given to me: in little things, in my use of money, and in faithfully and carefully using something that belongs to another?

2. In these three key areas, will You show me where I have done well and where I need to improve?

The Beatitudes and the Woes *(Matthew 5:1–11; 23:13–29; Luke 6:20–26)*

1. Jesus, as I slowly read the Beatitudes, will You show me how I fulfill these ways of living? Will You show me areas in which I need to improve?

2. Jesus, are there any of the woes that should convict me? Will You show me and guide me in what I need to do about them?

Over the next several days, return to your notes until you feel they are easy to recall, to experience, and have been built into your practice of life. If you were in a group, recall the things said together or to you. Ask the Lord to highlight the things that He wants you to meditate on.

Jot down thoughts as you do so:

Group Discussion

Giftings and Manifestations in the Body

Look at what you wrote in your Individual Study for your consideration of the attitudes Paul describes in 1 Corinthians 12:12–27.

1. Discuss together both the set of bad attitudes and the set of healthy attitudes.

2. Have you been guilty of, or seen, such bad attitudes in the Church? What are some reasons those attitudes seem to exist?

3. What are ways the good attitudes described by Paul can be fostered in your personal relationships and your relationships within your church?

Jesus and His Word

Review the various roles of Jesus given in the section "Connecting with Jesus and His Word" above. For each of the five Scripture verses about the role of Jesus, discuss together what you saw in the five verses reproduced below. Jot down any additional insights gained from the group.

1. "Teaching them to follow all that I have commanded you; and behold, I am with you always, to the end of the age" (Matthew 28:20).

2. "For where two or three have gathered in My name, I am there in their midst" (Matthew 18:20).

3. "I have been crucified with Christ; and it is no longer I who live, but Christ lives in me; and the life which I now live in the flesh I live by faith in the Son of God, who loved me and gave Himself for me" (Galatians 2:20).

4. "I can do all things through Him who strengthens me" (Philippians 4:13).

5. "For this purpose I also labor, striving according to His power which works mightily within me" (Colossians 1:29).

Connecting with Jesus' Parables

Discussing specific parables works well in a group setting as the depth and various viewpoints hidden within the parable more readily come to light.

Each parable focuses on a particular issue that Jesus wanted to address in the lives of His followers. In the group setting, take turns sharing answers to the questions about one of the parables. Then provide space for the group members to ask clarifying questions and receive the benefit of each other's thoughts.

The Father and Life

If you look at the calling on the life of almost any God-chosen biblical character, you will see that same amazing expression of God's desire and plan to be with us. In the calling of Abraham (Genesis 15:1), Jacob (Genesis 31:3), Moses (Exodus 3:12), Joshua (Joshua 1:5), Nehemiah (Nehemiah 2:8), Isaiah (Isaiah 41:10), David (Psalm 23:4), Solomon (1 Chronicles 28:20), the disciples (Mark 16:20), early Christians (Acts 11:21), and us forever (Matthew 28:20; John 17:20), each is told, "My chosen one whom I love. You are called according to My purpose. I'll be with you wherever you go."

The Spiritual Gifts Blueprint, chapter 7

Before you begin, please read chapters 7 and 8 of *The Spiritual Gifts Blueprint*.

Review of Last Session

Take a couple of minutes to review what you wrote in Session 5. Write one line that describes something that stood out to you. If you're in a group, share what you wrote, and observe the similarities or differences among your group's comments. Jot down any additional insights you gained from the group.

The Main Thing

This section covers the third "leg on the table" of the four-part spirit structure laid out by Paul in 1 Corinthians 12. Recall in verse 6 that he wrote, "There are varieties [*diairesis*] of effects [*energema*], but the same God who works all things in all persons."

All things in all persons. All. All. That role of the Father is described in chapters 7 and 8 of the book. Chapter 7 is designed to be a clear description of the Father's role, while chapter 8 is designed for personal application in both drawing near to the Father and in increasing our ability to distinguish Him as He interacts, mostly behind the scenes, in our lives and on our behalf.

Individual Study—Your Picture of the Father (Part 1)

Recall that Scripture is clear that each member of the Trinity intends to accompany you as you live your life. We have looked at intimacy with the Holy Spirit and Jesus in previous chapters. And for most people, those ideas are not difficult. In particular, Jesus is easy to envision from the gospel stories. His gentle character in drawing children to Himself and His understanding and desire to draw near to sinners are very attractive. As long as I'm not being a money changer in the temple, I'm good with Jesus.

But the Father? Hmmm. For many, the idea of the Father being intimate with us may feel a bit foreign, even scary. I may not be sure I have a place to put that. Getting that relationship transformed and rightly aligned is foundational to Christian life and living. Let's explore that first.

In chapter 8, page 122, I ask the question, Who is the Father to me? In that section, I describe an exercise that many have found very helpful in quickly zeroing in on a preliminary answer to that question. I say preliminary because, in hundreds of examples, when we actually consider where our picture came from and the great difference between that internal picture and the reality of the Father's character and love for us as repeatedly illustrated in Scripture, a light goes on. Here is that exercise from the book:[1]

> Here is the warmup. Close your eyes, take your time, and imagine your favorite drink. Just sit with that picture for a moment. You can probably describe it in detail—the frosty glass, the bubbles, the straw,

---

1. Thanks to my ministry partner, Jennifer Barnett, for this exercise.

the lemon slices, a mint leaf. You might even begin to smile or see yourself taking a sip. Mmm. Easy to see your drink, huh? We are using one of our three inner screens (the screen of imagination and impression) to visualize—to image.

We can invite God to connect within us using that screen. For example, many of the Psalms are David's internal pictures on that screen in his spirit that were given by God and written into a song. Psalm 23 is a classic. The Lord is my shepherd. He leads me beside quiet streams. He sets a table for me in the presence of my enemies.

Christian "mystics" are known for their use of this screen. But using it is not mystical; it is human. And it is God-created to allow Him to visually enter from the realm of the Spirit into our minds and thus into our conscious senses. The process of Him entering our minds and onto this screen is one of the main ways we hear God. And it is easy, and even naturally supernatural once we get used to the idea.

Ready? Close your eyes again, still your mind, and imagine listening to me as I say these words: "God the Father." Without slipping into analysis, what feeling, sense, memory, picture, or words come immediately to mind? Pause just a moment. Feel them.

Can you describe your inner picture? See if you can answer the questions below.

1. What did God the Father initially look like and feel like?

2. Where were you in that picture?

3. What feelings did you experience?

While there are many responses to the question (and none are wrong), by far the most common picture is of a white-haired, god-like being far away in the clouds—often faceless, but rarely seeming to notice you. Many see Abraham Lincoln as sculpted in Washington, D.C., sitting with a stern expression and staring off at some important problem—a great man but a bit intimidating.

An important question to ask yourself is, How does your picture of the Father seem to square with the reality of Scripture? And eventually, we'll want to know where that inner idea and picture of God the Father came from. How did you land on that impression?

Hold those questions, and let's go together on a journey to find the real Father by looking at: (1) examples of His invitation into partnership; (2) examples of His scripturally described role in your life; and, (3) His three-part destiny guarantee.

1. Examples of the Father's Invitation

Recall the story told in chapter 7 of the couple being called to Africa. They had a clear understanding that the Father never sends someone somewhere while simply hoping they make out okay. He invites them as partners and as adopted sons and daughters into His work. There are many stories in the Old Testament that are examples of this idea. Let's look at just a few. In each verse, look carefully at the promises or facts given and express them in your own words.

Abraham (see Genesis 15:1ff):

Moses (see Exodus 3:10ff):

David (see Psalm 23):

The Disciples (see Mark 16:20):

Early Christians (see Acts 11:21):

1. When you look at the Scripture passages above, what sort of common factors or similarities can you see?

2. How does what you see compare to your sense or picture of the Father?

3. If that was you interacting with God (instead of the various Bible characters), how might you feel after hearing God's words or seeing His actions?

2. Examples of the Father's Role

In chapter 7, I spoke of the two-fold overall role of the Father in your life: powerful and effective *steering* and *enabling*. He guides and resources us at exactly the right time and in the perfect way to fit each learning style, personality, circumstance, and maturity—yet His work is most often done quietly and behind the scenes.

Stop for a minute, close your eyes, and think of a very good Father who loves to interact with you intimately in those two ways. Can you recall times in your life when you needed those? Even now, how might that kind of support be welcome? Where are you wandering and need some help with steering? Where do you feel inadequate and need some help with enabling?

Scripture gives many examples of this way of the Father. In chapter 8, starting on page 127, I have provided some key topical examples demonstrating the Father's work. Let's take a look at each of them and get a good feel for how they may have, and can, work in your life.

For each of the Scripture verses given below, respond to the following questions:

1. How would you describe the issue or topic in your own words? Do any other verses or Bible stories come to mind when you think about the verse?
2. Describe what Scripture says in these verses about the Father's role in steering and enabling under this topic. What might your responsibility be?
3. As you look back over your Christian life, can you describe a memory of a way the Father may have assisted in steering and/or enabling you?

Topic 1: Things Working—God Working Things (see Romans 8:28)

Topic 2: Trials and Temptations (see 1 Corinthians 10:13)

Topic 3: Confession and Forgiveness (see 1 John 1:9)

Topic 4: Exchanged Anxiety (see Philippians 4:6–7)

Topic 5: Work and Reward (see Colossians 3:23–25)

3. The Father's Three-Part Guarantee

Many of us have life insurance policies. But this is far different. This is a "life assurance" policy! The Father's three-part guarantee concerning your life is given in three related verses reproduced here:

You will be like Him.

"For those whom He foreknew, He also predestined to become conformed to the image of His Son, so that He would be the firstborn among many brothers and sisters" (Romans 8:29).

You will be with Him.

"He predestined us to adoption as sons and daughters through Jesus Christ to Himself, according to the good pleasure of His will" (Ephesians 1:5).

You will share all His stuff.

"In Him we also have obtained an inheritance, having been predestined according to the purpose of Him who works all things in accordance with the plan of His will" (Ephesians 1:11).

1. Let's dream of heaven for a moment. Try to envision what these unconditional promises might look and feel like on that day. Imagine what each promise might mean to you.

2. Why do you think God placed these three promises in Scripture? When you think of a good earthly father, are there similar things he might say to you as you grow up or go off to college or start a new job?

3. As you read about God's three-part guarantee and think about your own uncertainty or anxiety in these areas, are there ways these promises bring peace, confidence, and relief? Which of them feels the most surprising or fulfilling? Why?

Individual Study—Your Picture of the Father (Part 2)

Let's return to the exercise of picturing the Father. But before you do, take a few minutes to do a quick review of what you have learned in the previous subsection.

1. What are some ways the three summaries about Father God given above (the Father's role, invitation, and three-part guarantee) changed your idea or knowledge of the Father? What felt most important to you?

2. With a clearer and more scriptural idea in mind of who the Father really is, let's return to the exercise from part 1. Close your eyes and listen again as I say the words, "God the Father." Pay attention to your picture of the Father. Has it changed? If so, take time to think about the implications of the more accurate picture of the Father. Note your feelings. Be still and enjoy that picture.

If there still seems to be a sense of struggle or blockage in your connection with the Father (in seeing, sensing, or hearing), know that this issue is common. It is not a big or permanent problem. I have witnessed hundreds of people move through that. The source is typically the result of not understanding the Father's kind character and open invitation. And that lack of understanding often comes from a combination of not having heart knowledge of scriptural truth about His open invitation to us (as portrayed in the exercises above) and deeper hurts that we retain from other father figures in our lives. Those hurts can warp our picture of God the Father.

The first issue is often helped by understanding the generosity and kindness of the Father's "invitation for coffee." Slowly read the following three invitation verses and see yourself answering yes to them.

> Draw near to God and He will draw near to you (James 4:8 NKJV).

> Let us therefore come boldly to the throne of grace, that we may obtain mercy and find grace to help in time of need (Hebrews 4:16 NKJV).

> For you have not received a spirit of slavery leading to fear again, but you have received a spirit of adoption as sons and daughters by which we cry out, "Abba, Father!" (Romans 8:15).

The second issue can often be easily addressed with the help from others who understand practicing forgiveness, letting Jesus bear our sorrow, renouncing lies that warp our picture, and receiving the truth about the Father as portrayed above. Such ministry is beyond this study guide, but I refer to you www.freedomprayer.org. There you can receive more information, as well as free, gentle, and transformative help in this area.

Group Discussion

The two Individual Study subsections above have been developed to also be effective in group discussion. In a group setting, share your responses to the questions and provide feedback to each other. One person should serve as the facilitator.

Your Picture of the Father (Part 1)

An effective way to discuss these concepts with each other in a group setting is simply to ask the questions used in Your Picture of the Father in the Individual Study Part 1 section above. It can look like this:

71

The leader states:

Ready? Close your eyes, still your mind, and imagine listening to me as I say these words, "God the Father." Without slipping into analysis, what feeling, sense, memory, picture, or words come immediately to mind? Pause just a moment. Feel them.

Can you describe your inner picture? See if you can answer the questions below.

1. What did God the Father look like and initially *feel* like?

2. Where were you in that picture?

3. What were your feelings?

4. Ask each person if they have any thoughts or insights about where their picture of the Father may have come from. What were their major influences?

Character and Ways of the Father

In a group setting, review the directions and responses to the three sections above that led through Examples of the Father's Invitation, Examples of the Father's Role, and The Father's Three-Part Guarantee.

1. Lead a discussion of responses to each section, share insights, and write down thoughts from others.

2. Discuss how these insights about the Father might influence or change their original picture or their beliefs of the Father. Write down insights.

Your Picture of the Father (Part 2)

Lead the group through a discussion of their responses to the drawing near exercise. Focus on the meaning and personal application of the three Scripture verses given in step 1. Encourage each one to describe his or her experience.

Discuss any blockage or persistent sense of distance. Discuss together particular insights about pictures of God the Father compared to the truth shown in Scripture. Pray for each other.

If a specific lie that was believed about God the Father emerges during the discussion, here is a quick and decisive declaration to get rid of it. The leader can lead the person in this declaration:

Father God, I believed that You were _____ , but I see that is incorrect. Today I renounce that belief and declare that _____ is true. Today I choose to reject the lies about You. Please help me to walk in that belief, and show me more of who You really are.

Your new freedoms in intimacy with Father God will be tested by the evil one, so spend time praying for each other. It would also be good to connect throughout the week to help each other walk out their declarations.

And remember this sure thing promise: "For I am confident of this very thing, that He who began a good work among you will complete it by the day of Christ Jesus" (Philippians 1:6).

The Holy Spirit and Manifestations

What I think Paul is saying is that the Holy Spirit distributes manifestations as He sees fit—and that, in Paul's own analysis, there are nine basic categories of these manifestations. Like *charisma* gifts, these are best thought of as points along a continuum, markers for clarity rather than limitations on variability—the "primary colors" of manifestations.

The Spiritual Gifts Blueprint, chapter 9

Before you begin, read chapters 9 and 10 of *The Spiritual Gifts Blueprint*.

Review of Last Session

Take a couple of minutes to review what you wrote in Session 6. Write one line that describes something that stood out to you. If you are in a group, share what you wrote, and observe the similarities or differences among your group's comments. Jot down any additional insights you gained from the group.

The Main Thing

In the last six chapters, I laid out the current situation in the Church concerning spiritual gifts and the first three parts of the Trinity-empowered grace structure (*pneumatikos*) for each believer: my basic gifting (*charisma*) and the Holy Spirit; my Kingdom ministry (*diakonia*) and Jesus; and the enabling and steering presence (*energema*) of the Father. This chapter focuses on the last piece of the four-part grace package, the manifestations (*phanerosis*) of the Holy Spirit. Paul is finally arriving at his answer to the question the Corinthians probably asked concerning the proper and orderly use of manifestations within their gatherings—and probably their lives. The details of his answer are found in 1 Corinthians chapters 12–14.

The Nine Manifestations: Introduction

Let me state three important points to serve as a backdrop for further individual and group study. They may save you some confusion and trouble. Trust me, I've made most of the mistakes!

1. The nine manifestations of the Holy Spirit in 1 Corinthians 12 are often called "the gifts (*charisma*) of the spirit" by various churches. And it is easy to understand that idea. If, however, we look at where Peter and Paul focus the use of the term *charisma*, it is the seven gifts in Romans 12 that are their target. When we use *charisma* for both gifts and manifestations, confusion is inevitable. That confusion has led directly to the disempowering situation described in chapter 1. Please read Appendix A in the book for a more detailed discussion of that term and my conclusions. Let's follow Paul's most clear usage of the term "gifts" and use the term "manifestations" (*phanerosis*) for the nine Spirit-empowered practices in 1 Corinthians 12 from here on out. Okay?

2. It is important to understand that manifestations are generally occurrences in time, like a thunderclap or a bird call. Some manifestations can be partially or fully *at-will*. Those manifestations are more widely distributed in churches worldwide. Personal tongues, spoken of in 1 Corinthians 14:18–19, 28, is an example, meaning that a believer can pray or speak in tongues whenever they desire. Some other manifestations may be *partially at will*, in that an

experienced believer can influence them to arise with growing frequency within or through themselves through confident expectation.

3. Understand that the Holy Spirit distributes (the word is *diairesis*) manifestations as He wills. It is not always easy to understand why certain individuals seem to be used by the Holy Spirit in certain ways, but it is clear that mature character is not always necessary—thus the Corinthian problems; however, the more powerful manifestations tend to most often accompany the more mature believers actively sharing the Gospel. It was that way in Acts and in Church history. Faith is often involved in some way, and stories in Scripture refer to its importance. Even Jesus couldn't work mighty miracles in His own hometown due to their active unbelief (see Mark 6:5; Matthew 13:58).

So let's live in a way that asks God for an increase in manifestations to support His Gospel and His will in any situation, and that is expectant. I have seen how that kind of Kingdom-focused living brings results. Got it? Let's move forward confidently, but not brashly.

Individual Study

Manifestation Definitions and Examples

Like *charisma* gifts, manifestations are best thought of as points along a continuum, markers for clarity rather than limitations on variability—the list of nine in 1 Corinthians 12:8–10 being sort of the "primary colors" of manifestations in a manner similar to *charisma* gifts. Below is an exercise to gain a clear definition and initial understanding of each of the manifestations.

1. Before you review the definition of manifestations, what is your current belief and understanding concerning manifestations? Where did that belief come from, and what influenced it?

2. Read and think briefly about the definitions and structure discussion of manifestations given in three places in the book:

   • A brief definition of the manifestations begins on page 140.
   • Manifestations of the Spirit: Organization, beginning on page 148, gives clarity on their relationship with each other.
   • Appendix D on page 210 gives a more detailed definition.

   To help make it your own,

   a. Read the biblical examples below and, in your own words, write a one-sentence definition of each manifestation.
   b. In the book of Acts references given below, give a short three- to five-word description of what it actually looked like.
   c. If you have experienced or seen this manifestation, give a one-sentence account of what you saw. Does what you saw seem to correspond with the definition and examples in Scripture?

   (Note: There can be a wide variation in how manifestations are expressed across the Church, including some "style copying" within denominations and locations).

Various Kinds of Tongues (see Acts 2:4; 10:46; 19:6)

The Interpretation of Tongues (see Acts 2:8; 10:46)

Prophecy (see Acts 7:2; 11:28; 13:2; 19:6; 21:4, 11)

The Word of Knowledge (see Acts 5:3; 8:26; 9:10; 10:5; 16:6–7, 9; 18:9; 20:23; 23:11; 27:10, 23)

The Distinguishing of Spirits (see Acts 8:21; 13:9–10; 16:16; 17:16; 19:17; 22:21)

The Word of Wisdom (see Acts 3:24; 6:10; 9:15; 10:15; 13:46; 14:22; 15:28; 17:22; 21:23; 22:21; 23:6)

Gifts of Healings (see Acts 3:6; 5:16; 9:18, 34; 14:10; 19:11; 28:8–9)

The Effecting of Miracles (see Acts 5:12; 6:8; 8:6; 9:40; 14:3; 16:26; 19:11; 20:10; 28:6)

Faith (see Acts 4:19, 29; 7:56; 14:9)

Balance in the Use of Manifestations

Read the final chapter section on *balance* beginning on page 153. Imbalance in understanding and practice in the use of manifestations has been a divisive issue in the Church. And, due to their sometimes seemingly unattractive nature, that imbalance has put manifestations effectively out of the reach of many. To combat this, Paul, in his guidance to Timothy in 2 Timothy 1:7, gives us a key truth and a pattern for our own balance and practice concerning manifestations. Recall from the book the example of the tripod and the three legs mentioned: power, love, and a sound mind. Both in *charisma* gifting and *phanerosis* manifestations, those three elements should be balanced.

Think of your place in the spectrum of churches that was presented in chapter 1. What is your history, practice, and balance? Think about each of the three parts of balance: power, love, and a sound mind. Think of how each of the three concepts plays a role in speaking in tongues or in speaking a prophetic word publicly or privately to someone. Ask the Father this question:

> *Lord, is there any imbalance in my (or my church's) understanding and practice of manifestations? If so, will You show me? Do I unwittingly have a short or a long leg?*

Jot down your thoughts.

If you sense there has been an area of imbalance in your walk, like the action taken in renouncing a false picture of the Father in Session 6, you can simply identify, ask what is true, and renounce your missteps.

> *God, I believed something false concerning Your manifestations of the Spirit. I believed that* _____ *, but I see that is incorrect. Today I give up that belief and I declare* _____ *is true. And today I choose to reject the untruths about Your manifestations. Please help me, God, to walk in a truer belief, and please lead me as I seek to obey You in this area.*

The Five Keys to Manifestations

Look at the Five Keys to Manifestations beginning on page 143 and read the descriptions carefully. These keys help attain and maintain that proper balance of power, love, and a sound mind concerning manifestations.

1. In the space after each key below, in your own words, write a one to two-sentence understanding of each key.
2. Look at these "key" questions:

   Have I misunderstood or neglected this key in the past? If so how?

   How might this key, if put into my life, have an impact on my belief system and practices as a Christian?

   How might this key, if put into my life, have an impact on my relationships?

3. Think of any practical decisions you can make or practical steps you can take to better live within that key or walk that key out.

Key 1: Humility and Lack of Show

Key 2: Owners and Users of Manifestations

Key 3: Unpredictability of Manifestations

Key 4: A Faith Atmosphere

Key 5: Filling with the Holy Spirit and Manifestations

Man's Makeup and Manifestation History

Sorry. You have homework reading. Make sure you read the sections of chapter 10 entitled Man's Makeup and Manifestations Through the Ages. I debated putting them into an appendix, but I felt strongly that these two concepts are very important in providing stabilizing insights and the truth necessary to undergird something that may feel strange or new.

Here are a few passages and questions to consider by yourself or together with a group:

1. Read 1 Thessalonians 5:23 about Paul's description of man's makeup.
   - Is the idea of man being comprised of spirit, soul, and body new to you?

   - What is your understanding of the key roles of each?

   - When you read of Jesus speaking of the *flow* of the Spirit coming out of your spirit (see John 7:38–39), how does that influence your understanding of the importance of your spirit and its interaction with the rest of your makeup?

2. Read Paul's description of the three kinds of people: fleshly (body driven), natural (soul led), and spiritual (spirit led) on pages 162 and 163.
   - From that description, think about different parts of your daily life. Can you identify the different motivations at work in your decision making?

- Does the spirit man's priority for conscience, intuition, and communion with God seem a bit foolish or mystical to you? If so, why? How might living more that way have an impact on your observations from the bullet point above?

3. Read Romans 8:1–17 to see Paul's detailed description of two lifestyles, the fleshly and the spiritual—of two kinds of men.
   - Note that his requirement for transitioning into a spiritual (*pneumatikos*) man is simple: set your mind on the flow of the Spirit from within your own spirit.
   - Use the strength and power of the Spirit and your spirit to put to death the power of the flesh in your life.

   In your own words, describe what that might look like in your life. Is there anything that seems too strange, mysterious, or hard about that? Why do you think it feels that way?

4. We see in Acts that tongues and prophecy often erupted from those who had just been filled with the Holy Spirit. Why do you think this happened? What purpose or benefit might they provide?

5. We also see how tongues survived in various places and ways through the ages. Since the charismatic movement of the 1970s, it is very common. If you do not speak in tongues, are you familiar with friends or churches that speak in tongues? What are your current thoughts about that manifestation?

Tongues and Prophecy Introduction

My goal in chapter 10 of the book was to demystify these two "introductory" manifestations (tongues and prophecy) and put them within easy reach of anyone interested. It was not to convince anyone they need to practice these two to become a better Christian.

I do ask, however, that you would temporarily set aside past beliefs and practices to let Scripture and the facts speak for themselves. I have seen that appropriately stepping into these manifestations, even with a bit of uncertainty, begins to open a door of an awakening of the human spirit within. Little else can do that in quite the same way. I have also seen the damage caused by misuse, hyper-spirituality, peer pressure, misunderstanding, or exaggeration of these two manifestations.

Let's invite the Holy Spirit into our inner dialog as we read and consider together.

Tongues

The *gift of tongues* has been a matter of Church debate since there was a Church. Certainly the Corinthians must have argued about it and its use.

A study of Church history will show that the idea of tongues and arguments about tongues popped up again and again. Early on, the debate was mostly about whether the miracle with tongues at Pentecost was in the speaking or the hearing. Scholars have come down on both sides.

Paul calls this manifestation "various kinds" of tongues. The word in Greek is *genos* and can mean "families," "groups," "orders," "classifications," "lineages," or "basic kinds." This definition by Paul leaves room for all sorts of classifications and occurrences. I have heard about and witnessed tongues being an unknown gibberish-sounding flow, a language unknown to the speaker but known to the hearer, beautiful singing, and a quiet under-the-breath prayer. Some ancient accounts are of saints speaking their own language but it being heard in multiple languages (which some say was the Pentecost experience).

Let's right-size our understanding of tongues based on two sources: the Word of God and observational evidence:

1. Read "A Summary of Paul's Teaching on Tongues" beginning on page 165. Under the heading "Facts about Tongues" is a list of eight things Paul says about the manifestation of tongues, followed by five things about their proper use within a church meeting. Let's make two summary lists:

   • In your own words, what are the top *four* good or positive things you can say about tongues?

• In your own words, what are the top *two* cautions or points of guidance that are important to help avoid misuse?

2. Read "Scientific Evidence" beginning on page 167.
   • What scientific facts about tongues are most surprising or enlightening to you?

   • What scientific facts about tongues are most supportive of the way tongues are described by Paul?

Tongues: Practical Application

If you wanted to experiment with tongues, the book provides a practical way to begin. The best way to do this is with a mature believer who has practiced tongues for some time and has a balanced understanding of the manifestation. But that is not required.

Begin to pay attention to your inner thoughts about tongues. Talk to friends about it. If you feel led to speak in tongues, a proven approach that is not manipulative or too challenging is to use the steps given on page 171 that are reproduced below:

1. Settle your heart and mind and ask God's Spirit to fill you for His purposes and the purpose of praise.
2. Begin to praise Him without self-consciousness.
3. When brain-formed words seem as if they are not enough, simply (and non-self-consciously) let the river flow.
4. It may trickle at first but don't stop!! Stay with it for ten or fifteen minutes at least.

Then return to it often. During the next few weeks, it will stabilize and become more and more uplifting. Keep this practice to yourself for a while. Let your consciousness of the flow gain ascendency in your life. It may, over time, sound different as you sense you are praying for different things or if you are simply praising. Mine do. See if Paul isn't right.

Don't be afraid.

Prophecy

The discussion of prophecy begins in the book on page 171. Many believers have an Old Testament idea of prophecy and prophets. You know, a fiery old guy with a beard and white hair calling down fire on sinners and foretelling the future. And they were killed if they were wrong—or right.

Paul seemingly redefines prophecy for New Testament use. "The one who prophesies speaks to people for their strengthening, encouraging and comfort" (1 Corinthians 14:3 NIV). Look up the meaning of these three words at BibleHub.com. Provide the Greek word and a concise definition of each of the three:

1.

2.

3.

Who wouldn't want those things spoken to them, especially if there was a strong element of God leading them to do so? Who wouldn't want to be a friend whom God uses to speak such encouragement to others? Even Paul, in 1 Corinthians 14, urges us all to prophecy.

First, let's clear up a misunderstanding. When specifically led by the Spirit, Christians can sometimes still "foretell the future." In Paul's multicolored analysis of manifestations of the Spirit, he has called knowing something through revelation a "word of knowledge" to differentiate that idea from prophecy. Old Testament prophets did both. So can you. Paul just divided the manifestation so that we could more easily understand the breadth of diversity in manifestations. The same is true with the word of wisdom.

New Testament prophecy is for everyone, not just a few (see 1 Corinthians 14:5) and is best used outside of a church setting. In that environment, people don't expect to sense the warm encouragement of God spoken to them by a normal person going about their lives. It is the lifeblood of the Church—and relationships of all types. In fact, I think this is what Paul meant in Ephesians 4:15 when he referred to "speaking the truth in love" through ligament relationships as described in Session 5.

It is one of God's main means of spreading personal encouragement to every part of the Body and to those who feel they are strangers to God. (See sample language below on ways to do so appropriately).

Read the following verses. In your own words, explain what truth they give about prophecy and why that truth might be necessary:

John 10:4–5 (hearing God)

Ephesians 4:29–30 (not grieving the Holy Spirit with our
words, which also applies to giving a prophecy)

1 Thessalonians 5:19–21 (receiving a prophecy)

1 Corinthians 13:9 (we prophesy in part)

1 Corinthians 14:29–33 (prophesy in meetings)

Read the section in the book on personal application beginning on page 176.

- Make a list in your own words of the key truths and practical advice for how to give a prophecy.

- Make a list in your own words of the key truths and practical advice for how to receive a prophecy.

Prophecy: Practical Application

If you are interested in exploring the reality of New Testament prophecy for yourself or in your group, I have found the following steps and thoughts to be very effective. Try them yourself!

- Ask God to help you be someone who can, in humility, give His kind words of encouragement.
- Make a practice of staying connected with God. As you go about your day, keep an open channel.
- Ask God to show you someone He would like to encourage. Make a promise that if He shows you, you will cooperate with Him and find a nonreligious, nonthreatening, and nonshowy way to say something to the person. Remember that prophetic words are sometimes a feeling, a single word

that starts things, a picture, a sense of what they need, a feeling that God loves them, etc.

- Use nonreligious and non-self-promoting language. For example, say:
  - "When I saw you, I felt as if God wanted me to encourage you that He sees you and . . ."
  - "I just love this about you . . ."
  - "I wanted to tell you that I felt like God was whispering, 'Don't give up. I'm here beside you.'"
  - "I felt like God nudged me and asked me to let you know that He sees you and was the first one to weep."

- Hug. Smile. Separate gracefully. Make no future promises or continue the conversation in a way that would detract from what God wanted you to share.

Again, above all, do not be afraid to step out gently, quietly, and without show. Especially speak this way within your own ligament relationships.

Group Discussion

Manifestation Definitions and Examples

Review the Manifestation Definitions and Examples section in the Individual Study subsection. I recommend that each group member completes the Individual Study section above. Then, in a group setting, use the following for discussion:

1. Talk about your faith journey and where you currently stand concerning the idea of and use of manifestations. Talk about your experiences. Ask each other questions.

2. Share together what scares, attracts, or repels you. Perhaps focus on tongues and prophecy first.

3. Pray for each other, and encourage each other to move as God leads in a way that is biblical and God-connecting.

Balance in the Use of Manifestations

In a group setting:

1. Look at the three questions under the Individual Study and Balance section and discuss your responses with the group.
2. For question 3 of the Individual Study section, if there are several group members wanting to walk through the steps of moving toward a truer belief, see if there is comfort to do it together. Have someone lead all members in helping them put words to their desire to be free. Support one another.

The Five Keys to Manifestations

A group discussion of the Five Keys to Manifestations has the advantage here in that there can be a widening of our understanding as we gain other perspectives. In a group setting, discuss the keys and these three questions given in the above section and repeated here:

Have I misunderstood or neglected this key in the past? If so, how?

How might this key, if put into my life, have an impact on my belief system and practices as a Christian?

How might this key, if put into my life, have an impact on my relationships?

Jot down the insights you gained in the group under each key below.

Key 1: Humility and Lack of Show

Key 2: Owners and Users of Manifestations

Key 3: Unpredictability of Manifestations

Key 4: A Faith Atmosphere

Key 5: Filling with the Holy Spirit and Manifestations

Man's Makeup and Manifestation History

Read the introduction under the Individual Study subsection under Man's Makeup. Ensure the group is familiar with the sections mentioned in the book.

1. Look at the first three questions above in the Individual Study section of this Study Guide about 1 Thessalonians 5:23 (Paul's three kinds of people) and Romans 8:1–17 (about fleshly and spiritual people). Share your responses to those three questions and make note of the things that seemed new to most people.

2. Look at and discuss question 4 from the Individual Study section on Man's Makeup and Manifestation History (reproduced here):

> We saw in Acts that tongues and prophecy often erupted from those who had just been filled with the Holy Spirit. Why do you think this happened? What purpose or benefit might they provide?

3. Recall that John 7:38 discussed the flow of the Holy Spirit coming from within our spirit. Here is the complete quote from Jesus in John 7:37–39:

> Now on the last day, the great day of the feast, Jesus stood and cried out saying, "If anyone is thirsty, let him come to Me and drink. The one who believes in Me, as the Scripture said, 'From his innermost being will flow rivers of living water.'" But this He said in reference to the Spirit, whom those who believed in Him were yet to receive; for the Spirit was not yet given, because Jesus was not yet glorified.

> Recall in the book of Acts that those filled with the Holy Spirit began to speak in tongues and (some) prophesied. How might tongues and prophecy manifestations relate to the words of Jesus here?

Tongues

If you have not done so, read the Introduction to Tongues and Prophecy in the Individual Study section on this topic on page 86.

1. We each have our story, experiences, and feelings about all things of the Holy Spirit. As your group members feel comfortable, have each give their history, experiences, and current feelings about tongues.

2. In your group, discuss your responses to question 1 in the Individual Study section about the "facts about tongues" and "their proper use."

3. Which of Paul's list of facts about tongues were the most popular "top four" in the group? Why do you think that is so? Look at both Paul's list and your own to see if you can describe what this might look like in a church or a Bible study setting. How might it look in normal life outside of group meetings?

4. Discuss your group's response to question 2 in the Individual Study section on scientific evidence. What was surprising to you and the group? How might that evidence change your opinion or understanding of tongues?

5. What is the status and stance of the group members concerning tongues? Go around the room and ask each member to express their thoughts as they feel comfortable doing so.

6. Brainstorm thoughts about future interaction with the idea and practice of tongues. Read the Practical Application section starting on page 88. or in the book. What feelings does that description elicit?

Prophecy

Read the discussion of prophecy in the Individual Study section starting on page 89.

1. In the Individual Study section above, a series of verses about New Testament prophecy are listed and responses are requested. In the group, discuss your understanding and ideas about each of the verses and how each might be a puzzle piece of the whole.
2. The Prophecy: Practical Application section on page 92 discusses how to give or receive a prophecy. Read through that guidance together and discuss the key points. What sort of consequences might be experienced if the advice were violated or ignored?

Getting Started

1. *Groups.* There is an exercise for groups (the "hot seat") given in the book starting on page 182. It works very well. A high school had even incorporated "the cry thing" (as they called it) into their annual senior retreat.
2. Try the hot seat exercise in your group. Have fun and discuss feelings and the sense of the meanings of the words spoken. Be kind but tell the truth—always!

Remember Paul's words: "Follow the way of love and eagerly desire gifts of the Spirit, especially prophecy" (1 Corinthians 14:1 NIV).

Summing Things Up

It was 1988, and I was daydreaming and gazing out the window of a small twin-prop plane on approach to Nashville. Suddenly, a woman across the aisle shrieked, "The plane is on fire! The plane IS. ON. FIRE!" That is when I first learned about gifting and finding God's purpose for people's lives.

The Spiritual Gifts Blueprint, Introduction

Before you begin, read chapter 11 of *The Spiritual Gifts Blueprint*.

Review of Last Session

Take a couple of minutes to review what you wrote in Session 7. Write one line that describes something that stood out to you. If you are in a group, share what you wrote, and observe the similarities or differences among your group's comments. Jot down any additional insights you gained from the group.

The Main Thing

In the last seven chapters, we worked together through the main points given in the book. My hope is that you have gained valuable and practical understanding of the Holy Spirit and *charisma* gifting, about Jesus and *diakonia* ministry, about the Father and resourcing and enabling (*energema*), and about manifestations (*phanerosis*) and the Holy Spirit. In this chapter, I want to succinctly sum things up the way God did for me so many years ago—but without the fiery airplane and screaming.

Compact Truth

Ephesians 2:10 sums up most of what is contained between the covers of the book *The Spiritual Gifts Blueprint*. In this final section of the Study Guide, let's step away from digesting lots of information (fun as that is) and go in the opposite direction. Let's meditate on only one verse, and let its layered depth speak to us. Much of what this verse meant to me is found in chapter 11 of *The Spiritual Gifts Blueprint*. As you meditate on it, I am betting that you will hear and feel many other things as well.

> For we are His workmanship, created in Christ Jesus for good works, which God prepared beforehand so that we would walk in them.

Ephesians 2:10

Our Meditation

Recall that Jesus often said things to the scribes and Pharisees like, "Have you not read," or "It is written," and then quoted some little-known verse that caused every listener to smack their foreheads—or want to crucify Him.[1] The difference is not that He read it more carefully, but that He read it "in connection with" His Father and the Holy Spirit—who brought the Scripture passages to life and began to show Him their many layers of truth and application. Much of that insight probably happened years earlier when He was alone connecting and meditating with His Father (and yours!). Paul, too, spent years thinking about the deeper meanings of Old Testament verses he thought he knew well, and listening to God as He gave Paul New Testament truth to reflect the new age in the Church.

We can also receive truth and guidance from God as we approach Him, alone, connected, and still. Let's try it with Ephesians 2:10. First, we will break the text into short, logical segments or thoughts.

---

1. For example, Matthew 12:3; 19:4; 21:42; 22:31.

Then we will take time to connect internally and visually (on that internal screen of impression and imagination). Finally, we will take each segment and, like sucking on a good hard candy, let it play in our minds after asking, *Jesus (or God) is there anything You want to show me? I want to know You more.*

Things often begin to come into view on that inner screen of impression with memories, thoughts, insights, other verses, pictures, feelings, or just a sudden knowing and a wink. Let's try that with the verse above. No pressure. Rest and enjoy.

Individual Study: Ephesians 2:10

Take a few moments to still your thoughts and set aside the busyness and distractions ("Later!") and draw near to God. When you are ready, step into the Scripture meditation described below.

For each segment of Ephesians 2:10, let your mind's eye form both a picture and a set of ideas or facts that can be turned over and over. Let's do the first segment together. Then use the same approach for the other segments.

For We Are His Workmanship

Recall from chapter 11 that *workmanship* implies "craftsmanship." What can it mean that you (yes, you) are His craftsmanship? Your Holy Spirit–given *charisma* gift in you is perfectly cut, trimmed, sanded, and finished for its planned purpose. Perfectly! Can you see yourself being planned and slowly hand-crafted, fastened with dowels of oak, and finished smooth and strong?

- "For" refers back to the previous verses where we see God's immense mercy and love for us, His eternal plan, and His unmerited salvation. Camp on those for a time.
- I fit into His plan "for" I am His workmanship. I am His plan—not my plan and not Satan's plan. *His* plan. I am His eternal plan. Prepared both in me and for me. Wow!
- "Workmanship" refers to something that has been crafted, designed, and made for a specific purpose—perfect for that purpose. In a sense, I am "perfect" for my own life. Nothing is missing. I can't be disqualified. Even if I sin, I can confess my sin and return stronger.

- Romans 1:20 says that creation was also His workmanship and through it, we can understand His attributes and nature. Me, too!
- I am part of God's unchangeable, perfect, eternal plan. I've been given a part in that, and *I am perfect* for that part.

Okay. Your turn. Start with your own consideration of the first phrase. Let your imagination and impression screen light up. Read the verse in context again to see the immense backdrop in which this verse lives. Feel His smile. He loves warm humor and strong hugs. Go for it! Then move on to each of the other phases. Slowly!

For We Are His Workmanship (your turn)

Created in Christ Jesus

For Good Works

Which God Prepared Beforehand

So That We Would Walk in Them

Group Discussion: Ephesians 2:10

It is recommended that each group member complete the Individual Study section above. Alternately, the Individual Study section can be completed in a group setting. In such a setting:

1. Prior to reading the example meditation, ask the group to share their observations from the first segment, "We are His workmanship."
2. Review together the example given for the first verse segment, "We are His workmanship." Notice the varied thinking, imagery, and other verses. What things did the group bring up that were not in the example?

Go segment by segment doing the same meditation. Look for the following patterns or truths:

- the immensity and intimacy of God contained within this verse
- the work and the role of each member of the Trinity within it—*charisma, diakonia, energema,* and *phanerosis* all working differently, all working together
- the works are also prepared (how is that?)
- the end game for all of this—the action verb directed at you

For We Are His Workmanship (your turn)

Created in Christ Jesus

For Good Works

Which God Prepared Beforehand

So That We Would Walk in Them

Ongoing Study, Ongoing Growth

Thank you for working through the guide and the book! Whew!

This is just the beginning. After a few months, I encourage you to revisit your responses and your insights. Revisit the way the book may have changed your sense of destiny and purpose, your connection with each member of the Trinity, and your sense of yourself. Remember that you are someone of great worth in God's eyes—eternal worth—and someone who is entrusted with works prepared before the foundation of the world.

I think you might realize that understanding the concepts in this book places you right in front of an open door that cannot be shut by men or Satan, like the church in Philadelphia (see Revelation 3:8). You are now in a perfect place to understand that:

- His "workmanship" within you, your *charisma* gifting package, and other characteristics set you up to be looking in the right direction with ears that can hear.
- You were created in Christ Jesus, in the Body, connected to the Brain for a purpose—for good works; your purpose is to know Him and to work with Him on those good works—your *diakonia*.
- The Father chose you in Christ, in the Body, and prepared these works (*energema*) before the foundation of the world (see Ephesians 1:4), perfectly matched to your gifting, your calling, and your ability. And He is working behind the scenes to cause things to work together for your good. Why? Because knowing your gifting and the work of Christ through you, you are certainly called according to His purpose (see Romans 8:28).

- Your job is not to strive, not to grunt and push and moan— but simply to "walk in them." If you need a power push, it will be there (*phanerosis*). Walk. In. Them.

You are set up for a kind of success that is not able to be realized merely using your brawn, brains, and abilities. And you are invited to do all this with the Trinity—gentle and fiery Holy Spirit and His *charisma* gifting built inside of you, and His toolbox of *phanerosis* on loan for any job where a power tool is needed; brother Jesus and His *diakonia* plan—a string of assignments that will grow you up and fill you out; and loving Father and His *energema* causing things to happen, how and when you need them, in ways that are intended to cause you to smile and even laugh with joy.

In closing, I have listed a few verses in Ephesians that talk about that favor, eternal guarantee, and immense destiny. It takes what we have learned and casts it against the backdrop of eternity. We can say, as Paul did, that such knowledge is too great for us. You're all set. Go for it, my friend.

> Blessed be the God and Father of our Lord Jesus Christ, who has blessed us with every spiritual blessing in the heavenly places in Christ, just as He chose us in Him before the foundation of the world, that we would be holy and blameless before Him. In love He predestined us to adoption as sons and daughters through Jesus Christ to Himself, according to the good pleasure of His will, to the praise of the glory of His grace, with which He favored us in the Beloved. In Him we have redemption through His blood, the forgiveness of our wrongdoings, according to the riches of His grace which He lavished on us. In all wisdom and insight, He made known to us the mystery of His will, according to His good pleasure which He set forth in Him, regarding His plan of the fullness of the times, to bring all things together in Christ, things in the heavens and things on the earth. In Him we also have obtained an inheritance, having been predestined according to the purpose of Him who works all things in accordance with the plan of His will, to the end that we who were the first to hope in the Christ would be to the praise of His glory. In Him, you also, after listening to the message of truth, the gospel of your salvation—having also believed, you were sealed in Him with the Holy Spirit of the promise, who is a first installment of our inheritance, in regard to the redemption of God's own possession, to the praise of His glory.
>
> Ephesians 1:3–14

Andy Reese is a thankful follower of God, a lucky husband, a proud father and grandfather, an engineer, a writer, and a serial idea entrepreneur.

Professionally, he is a well-known thought leader in rainwater management and green sustainable design having co-authored *Municipal Stormwater Management* (Lewis Publishers, 2003). He taught at Vanderbilt and Lipscomb Universities and has given many national and international keynote addresses. He is the co-author of *Freedom Tools* (Chosen Books, 2015) and helps lead a multinational, nonprofit ministry (Freedom Prayer—www.freedomprayer.org) that seeks to help bring freedom and spiritual vitality to believers. He is the author of several other books and is the developer of "Magi," a presentation of the science, geography, history, and culture explaining the authenticity of the Star of Bethlehem story. This presentation has over 100,000 YouTube views.